D1235644

# Write me a Poem

## FINDING THE RHYME IN A POEM

by VALERIE BODDEN

Illustrations by MONIQUE FELIX

CREATIVE EDUCATION ■ CREATIVE PAPERBACKS

Published by Creative Education and Creative Paperbacks
P.O. Box 227, Mankato, Minnesota 56002
Creative Education and Creative Paperbacks are imprints of The Creative Company
www.thecreativecompany.us

Design and production by Chelsey Luther
Art direction by Rita Marshall
Printed in the United States of America

Photographs by Corbis (Corbis), DeviantArt (Esiri76). Illustrations © by Monique Felix.

Library of Congress Cataloging-in-Publication Data
Bodden, Valerie.
Finding the rhyme in a poem / Valerie Bodden.
p. cm. — (Write me a poem)
Includes index.
Summary: An elementary exploration of rhyme and rhythm in poetry, introducing syl-
lables, rhyme schemes, and sonnets as well as poets such as Elizabeth Barrett Browning.
Includes a writing exercise.
ISBN 978-1-60818-620-4 (hardcover)
ISBN 978-1-62832-252-1 (pbk)
ISBN 978-1-56660-680-6 (eBook)
1. Poetry—Authorship—Juvenile literature. 2. English language—Rhyme—Juvenile
literature. I. Title.

PN1059.R5B63 2015
808.1—dc23          2015007209

CCSS: RI.1.1, 2, 3, 5, 6, 7; RI.2.1, 2, 3, 5, 6, 7; RI.3.1, 3, 5, 7; RF.1.1; RF.2.3, 4; RF.3.3

First Edition HC 9 8 7 6 5 4 3 2 1
First Edition PBK 9 8 7 6 5 4 3 2 1

# Table of Contents

# Beat and Rhythm

YOUR favorite song comes on the radio. You start to dance. You sing along. You just love the sounds and the feel of the beat!

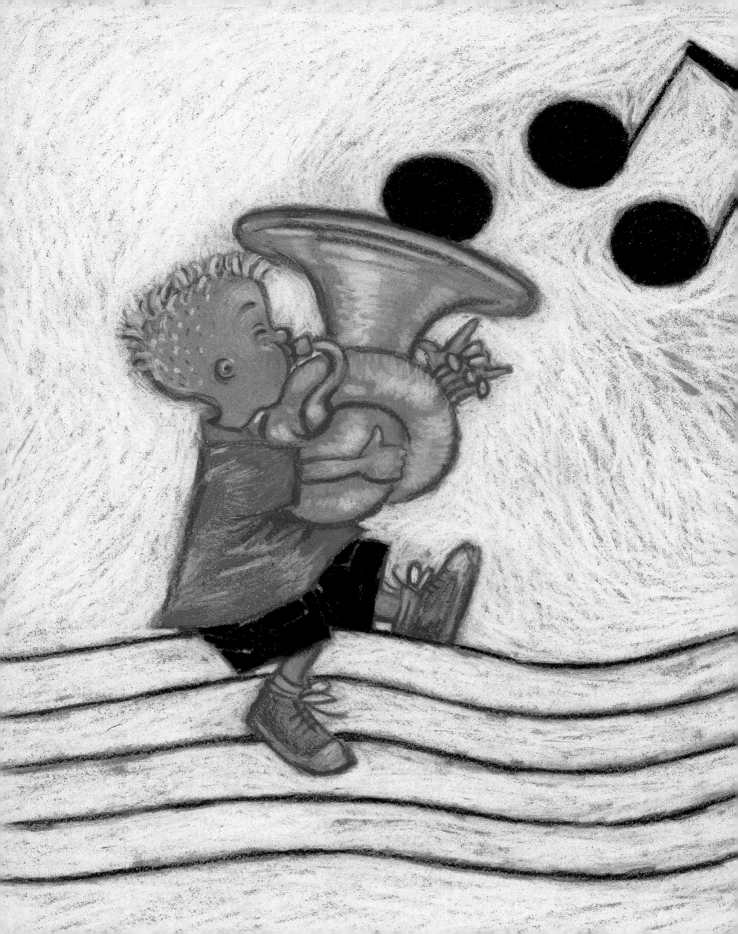

POEMS are a lot like music. When you read a poem, you can hear its **rhythm** (*RIH-thum*). In music, instruments or voices make the rhythm and keep the beat. But in poetry, rhythm is made by words.

# Same Sounds

When words <u>rhyme</u>, they end with the same sound. Sometimes poets use rhyme to make their poems sound more musical. Rhymes can make poems easier to remember, too. Notice the rhyming words at the ends of the lines in William Allingham's poem "Four Ducks on a Pond."

*Four ducks on a pond,*
*A grass-bank beyond,*
*A blue sky of spring,*
*White clouds on the wing;*

Listen for the "ahnd" and "ing" sounds.

# Rhyming Lines

A plan for a poem's rhyming lines is called its rhyme scheme (*SKEEM*). In "Four Ducks on a Pond," lines one and two rhyme. So do lines three and four. In other poems, the first line might rhyme with the third line. Can you figure out the rhyme scheme in "Windy Nights" by Robert Louis Stevenson?

*Whenever the moon and stars are set,*
*Whenever the wind is high,*
*All night long in the dark and wet,*
*A man goes riding by.*

# Strong Words

When we speak, we say some words or **syllables** more strongly than others. **Accented** and unaccented syllables help make rhythm, too. Listen for the rhythm in this line from Edgar Allan Poe's poem "The Raven."

* The pink words and syllables are accented.

Once upon a midnight dreary, while I pondered,
weak and weary

Try doing the opposite accents. How does that sound?

13

# Poetic Feet

In poetry, a group of accented and unaccented syllables is called a foot. An iamb (*EYE-am*) is a foot that has one short syllable and one long syllable (*bum-BUM*). Joyce Kilmer's "Trees" uses the *bum-BUM* rhythm four times in each line.

*I think that I shall never see
A poem as lovely as a tree.*

The short-long, short-long rhythm sounds like rocking back and forth.

# Finding Rhyme in Sonnets

Sonnets are poems with 14 lines. Each line of a sonnet uses the *bum-BUM* rhythm five times. Count the five feet in the lines from "The World Is Too Much with Us" by William Wordsworth.

*The world is too much with us; late and soon,*

*...*

*This Sea that bares her bosom to the moon;*
*The winds that will be howling at all hours*

Clap every time you say a word in pink.

The next time you read a poem, listen for its rhythm and its rhyme. You might even want to clap along to the beat!

# Famous Poet: Elizabeth Barrett Browning

# BRITISH

poet Elizabeth Barrett Browning was born in 1806. Many of her poems are about love, God, or **politics**. Listen for the rhyme and rhythm in these lines from Sonnet 43.

*How do I love thee? Let me count the ways.*

*…*

*I love thee with a love I seemed to lose*
*With my lost saints—I love thee with the breath,*
*Smiles, tears, of all my life!—and, if God choose,*
*I shall but love thee better after death.*

Elizabeth started writing poetry as a child.

# Activity:
# Write Me a Poem

# WRITE a four-line poem about

your favorite color. Make the last word in lines one and three rhyme. The last words in lines two and four should rhyme, too. Now read your poem out loud. Can you hear the rhythm?

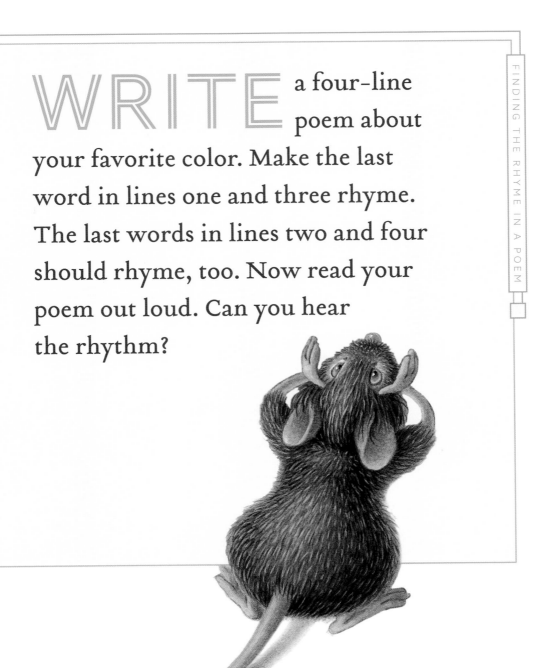

# Glossary

| | |
|---|---|
| **accented** | stressed; spoken more strongly than unaccented syllables |
| **politics** | the ideas and actions involved in running a government or controlling a country |
| **rhyme** | two or more words that end with the same sound |
| **rhythm** | the rising and falling sound in music or speech |
| **syllables** | parts of a word that are pronounced as one sound; most syllables are made up of at least one vowel (a, e, i, o, u) sound and might have one or more consonant sounds as well |